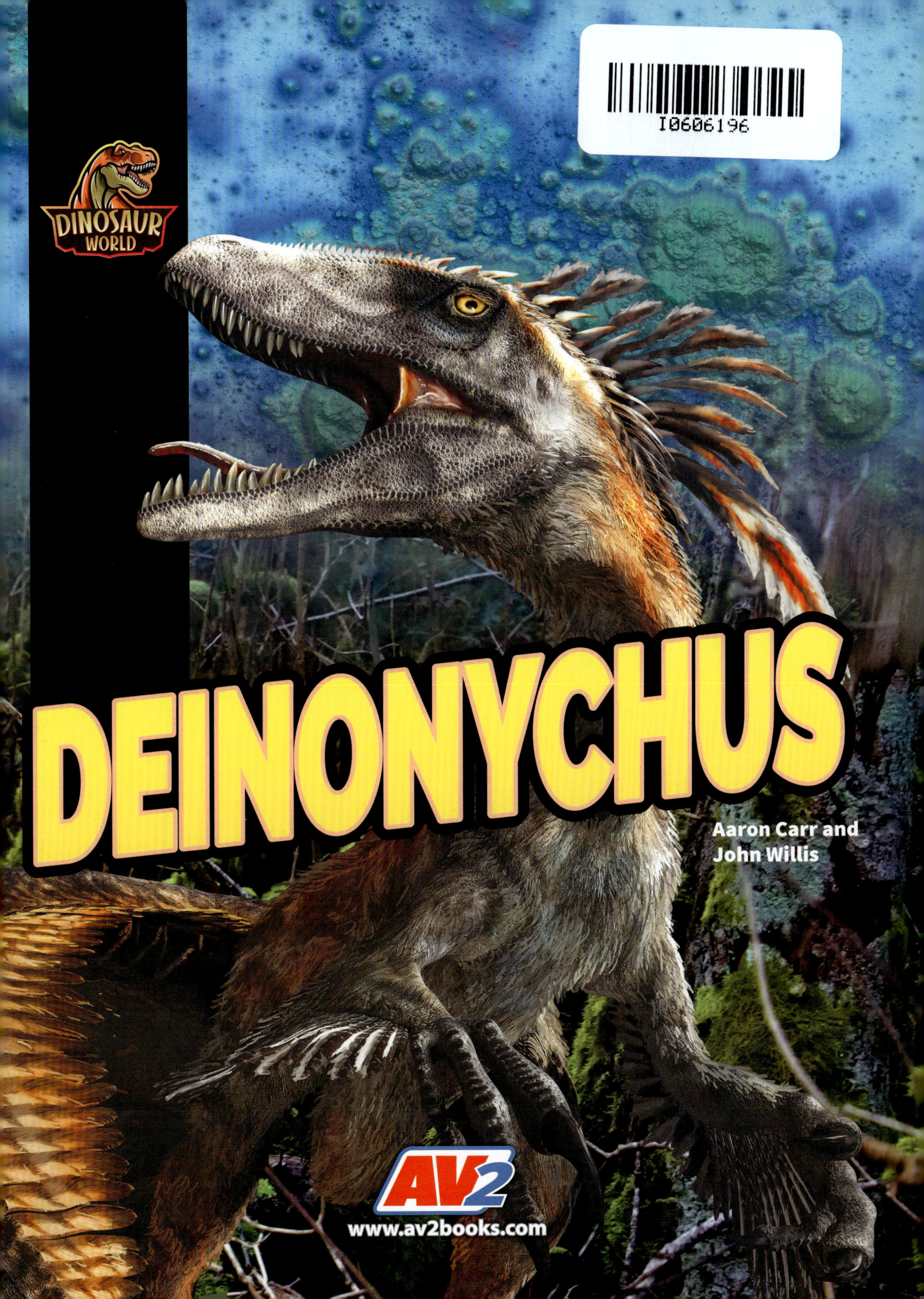
I0606196
DINOSAUR WORLD
DEINONYCHUS
Aaron Carr and John Willis
AV2
www.av2books.com

Step 1
Go to **www.av2books.com**

Step 2
Enter this unique code
FEXOVXMH8

Step 3
Explore your interactive eBook!

AV2 is optimized for use on any device

Your interactive eBook comes with...

Contents
Browse a live contents page to easily navigate through resources

Audio
Listen to sections of the book read aloud

Videos
Watch informative video clips

Weblinks
Gain additional information for research

Try This!
Complete activities and hands-on experiments

Key Words
Study vocabulary, and complete a matching word activity

Quizzes
Test your knowledge

Slideshows
View images and captions

This title is part of our AV2 digital subscription

1-Year Grades K–5 Subscription
ISBN 978-1-7911-3320-7

Access hundreds of AV2 titles with our digital subscription.
Sign up for a FREE trial at **www.av2books.com/trial**

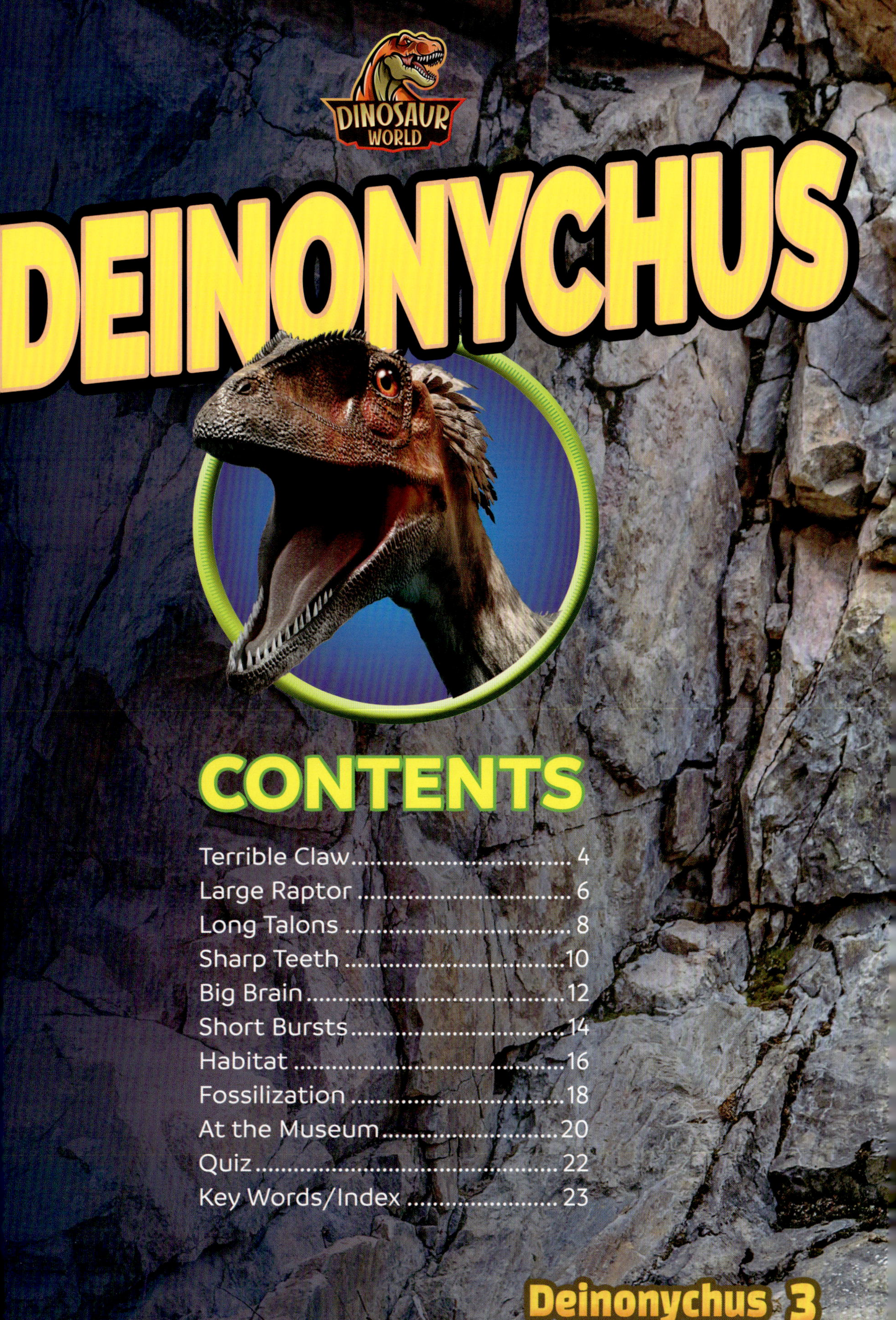

DEINONYCHUS

CONTENTS

Terrible Claw

Deinonychus was part of the dromaeosaur **family** of dinosaurs. Its name means "terrible claw." Dromaeosaurs were medium-sized, **bipedal** dinosaurs known for their speed and agility. These dinosaurs are often called raptors.

Deinonychus and other dromaeosaurs were likely covered in feathers. Many scientists believe these dinosaurs were the ancient ancestors of modern-day birds. *Deinonychus* served as the model for the raptors in the popular *Jurassic Park* movie series. However, the movies used the name of a different dromaeosaur, *Velociraptor*, instead.

Deinonychus

Large Raptor

Deinonychus was one of the larger dromaeosaurs. It was about 5 feet (1.5 meters) tall. This would have given *Deinonychus* a body about the size of a mountain lion, although the dinosaur's tail would have made it longer.

Deinonychus was much larger than *Velociraptor* and several other small dromaeosaurs. However, other dromaeosaurs, such as *Utahraptor*, could grow much larger.

Long Talons

Deinonychus had a long, sharp **talon** on each foot. The dinosaur's name comes from these talons, which were used for hunting. The talons were found on the second toe of each foot. A *Deinonychus* talon could be longer than a tiger's claw.

Deinonychus's talons were curved into a **sickle** shape. It held them off the ground when it was walking to avoid dulling their points. *Deinonychus* had much smaller claws on its other fingers and toes.

CLAW AND TALON COMPARISON
Velociraptor
2.5 inches (6.4 centimeters)
Tiger
4 inches (10.2 cm)
Deinonychus
5 inches (12.7 cm)

Sharp Teeth

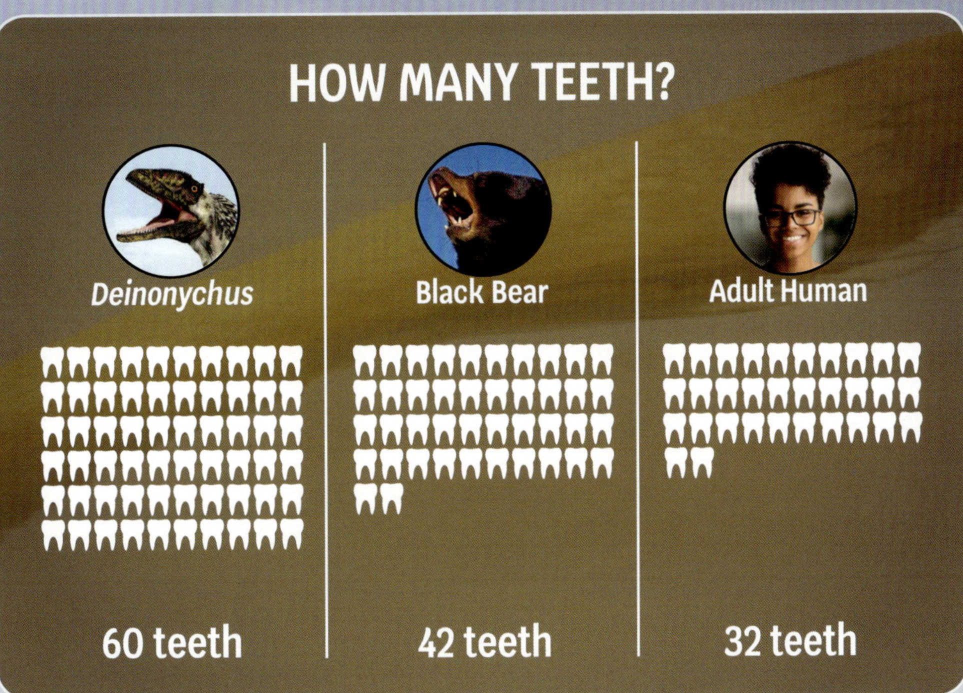

Deinonychus was a **carnivore**. It probably ate anything it could catch, ranging from small animals to dinosaurs much larger than itself. *Deinonychus* had many sharp teeth that pointed toward the back of its mouth. This helped *Deinonychus* keep its **prey** from getting away. The sharp teeth were also perfect for slicing through meat.

Deinonychus had long arms with three-fingered hands. It could move these fingers, and the sharp claws attached to them, to help capture and hold its food.

Big Brain

Deinonychus was likely one of the smartest dinosaurs that ever lived. It had a large brain compared to other dinosaurs. *Deinonychus* may have been able to put this intelligence to use when hunting. Evidence suggests that *Deinonychus* worked in **packs** to hunt larger dinosaurs, such as *Tenontosaurus*.

Short Bursts

No one can say for certain how quickly any dinosaur could move, but many scientists think dromaeosaurs were fairly speedy. However, while *Deinonychus* could walk quickly, it was likely not a fast runner.

The size and **proportions** of *Deinonychus*'s leg bones have led some scientists to believe it moved like a lion, using **agility** and short bursts of speed to capture prey. *Deinonychus* held its body in a **horizontal** position **parallel** to the ground. In this position, the dinosaur's long tail acted as a **counterweight** to help keep it balanced.

Habitat

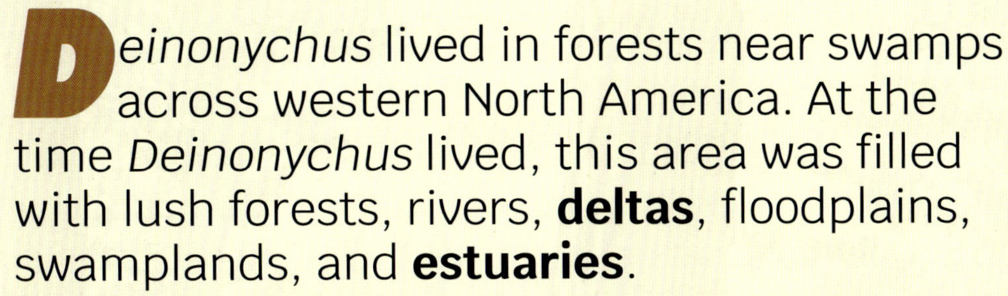

D*einonychus* lived in forests near swamps across western North America. At the time *Deinonychus* lived, this area was filled with lush forests, rivers, **deltas**, floodplains, swamplands, and **estuaries**.

Deinonychus's **habitat** was similar to many of the landforms found in Louisiana today. The plant life in this area supported the animals that *Deinonychus* preyed upon.

Fossilization

Deinonychus lived from about 150 million to 100 million years ago. This time was known as the Early Cretaceous Period. Everything that people know about *Deinonychus* has been learned by studying its bones, which turned into **fossils** over millions of years.

Steps of Fossilization

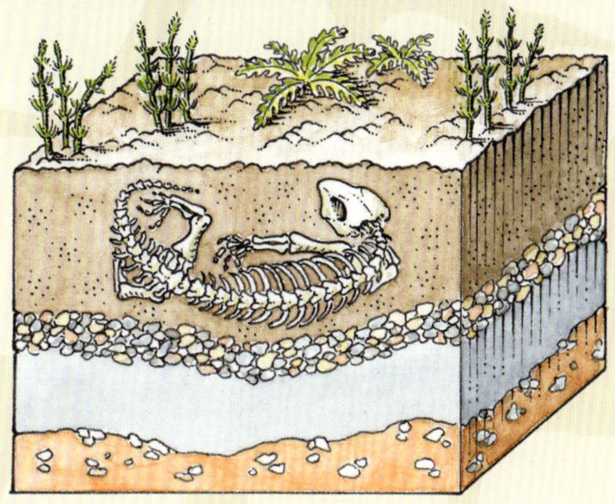

1 An animal dies and is quickly covered in sand, mud, or water. This keeps the hard parts of the body, such as bones, teeth, and claws, from **decomposing**.

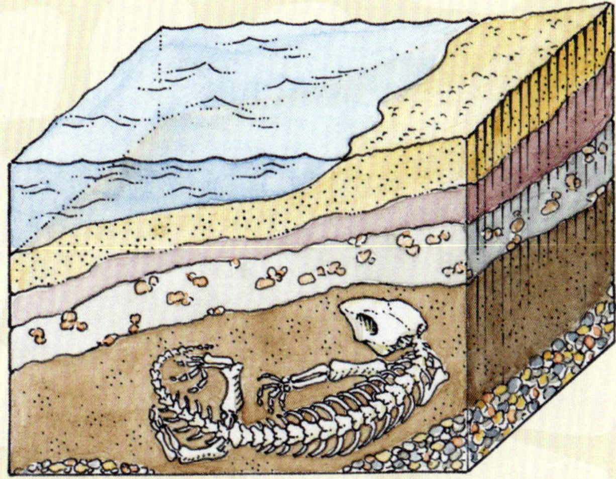

2 The body is pressed between layers of mud and sand.

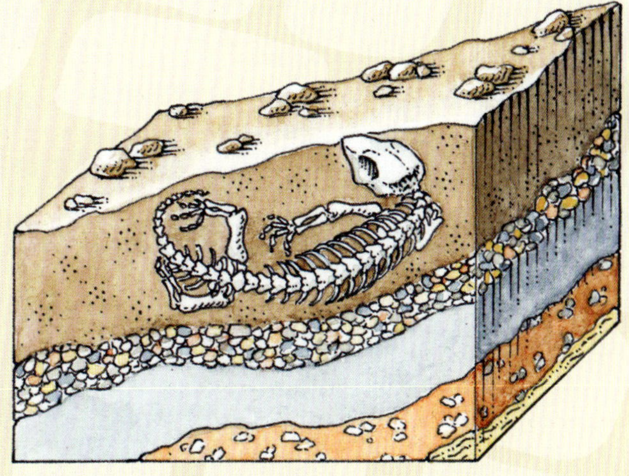

3 Over millions of years, the layers turn into stone. The animal's bones and teeth turn into stone as well. This **preserves** the animal's size and shape.

At the Museum

See For Yourself

Visitors to the American Museum of Natural History in New York City can see the world's only *Deinonychus* skeleton display made entirely of fossils.

People can go to museums to see fossils and learn more about *Deinonychus*. Millions of people around the world visit museums each year to see *Deinonychus* fossils in person.

Many large museums have permanent *Deinonychus* displays. These museums include the National Museum of Natural History in Washington, D.C. and the American Museum of Natural History in New York City.

Quiz

1
In which direction did a *Deinonychus*'s teeth point?

2
What does *Deinonychus* mean?

3
What was the largest dromaeosaur?

4
In which period did *Deinonychus* live?

5
How do scientists think *Deinonychus* was able to hunt larger dinosaurs?

6
Which toes held a *Deinonychus*'s long talons?

7
How did *Deinonychus*'s tail help keep it balanced?

8
Which U.S. state today has landforms similar to *Deinonychus*'s habitat?

ANSWERS
1. Toward the back of its mouth 2. "Terrible claw" 3. *Utahraptor* 4. Early Cretaceous Period 5. By hunting in packs 6. The second toe on each foot 7. By acting as a counterweight 8. Louisiana

Key Words

agility: the ability to move quickly and gracefully

bipedal: standing on two legs

carnivore: an animal that only eats meat

counterweight: a weight used to balance out another object

decomposing: breaking down or rotting

deltas: triangular pieces of land found at the mouths of rivers

estuaries: locations where rivers reach the ocean

family: a group of related plants or animals

fossils: remains from living things that have turned to stone over many years

habitat: the place where an animal naturally lives and grows

horizontal: when something is positioned from side to side instead of up and down

packs: groups of hunting animals

parallel: in the same direction as something but never touching it

preserves: stops something from decomposing

prey: animals hunted and eaten by other animals

proportions: the relationships between the size, number, and amount of a group of objects

sickle: a farming tool with a curved blade

talon: a sharp claw of an animal such as a bird

Get the best of both worlds.

AV2 bridges the gap between print and digital.

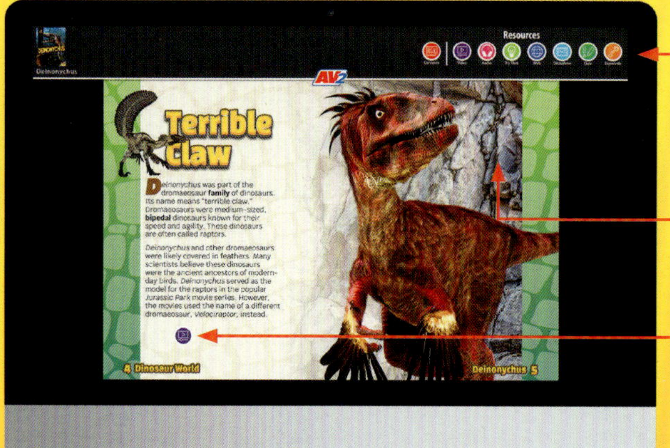

The expandable resources toolbar enables quick access to content including **videos**, **audio**, **activities**, **weblinks**, **slideshows**, **quizzes**, and **key words**.

Animated videos make static images come alive.

Resource icons on each page help readers to further **explore key concepts**.

Published by AV2
276 5th Avenue, Suite 704 #917
New York, NY 10001
Website: www.av2books.com

Library of Congress Control Number: 2020951586

ISBN 978-1-7911-3440-2 (hardcover)
ISBN 978-1-7911-3441-9 (softcover)
ISBN 978-1-7911-3442-6 (multi-user eBook)

Printed in Guangzhou, China
1 2 3 4 5 6 7 8 9 0 25 24 23 22 21

022021
101120

Designer: Terry Paulhus **Project Coordinator:** John Willis

Every reasonable effort has been made to trace ownership and to obtain permission to reprint copyright material. The publisher would be pleased to have any errors or omissions brought to its attention so that they may be corrected in subsequent printings.

AV2 acknowledges Getty Images, iStock, Newscom, Wikimedia, and Jon Hughes, pixel-shack.com, as the primary image suppliers for this title.